THE
INVENTION
OF THE
TELEPHONE

by Lucy Beevor

raintree 🍃

a Capstone company — publishers for children

Raintree is an imprint of Capstone Global Library Limited, a company incorporated in England and Wales having its registered office at 264 Banbury Road, Oxford, OX2 7DY – Registered company number: 66955

www.raintree.co.uk
myorders@raintree.co.uk

Text © Capstone Global Library Limited 2018
The moral rights of the proprietor have been asserted.

Edited by Jennifer Huston
Designed by Heidi Thompson
Original illustrations © Capstone Global Library Ltd 2018
Picture research by Eric Gohl
Production by Katy LaVigne
Originated by Capstone Global Library Ltd
Printed and bound in Inida.

Original Edition Author
Marc Tyler Nobleman

ISBN 978 1 4747 5284 8 (hardback)
22 21 20 19 18
10 9 8 7 6 5 4 3 2 1

ISBN 978 1 4747 5296 1 (paperback)
22 21 20 19 18
10 9 8 7 6 5 4 3 2 1

British Library Cataloguing in Publication Data
A full catalogue record for this book is available from the British Library.

Acknowledgements
Alamy: Chris Willson, 25, Chronicle, 22, Glasshouse Images, 20, Paul Fearn, 13, Science History Images, 11; Getty Images: Stringer/H. Armstrong Roberts, 21, Ted Soqui, 24, Time Life Pictures, 4, Universal History Archive, 12; Library of Congress: 23; Newscom: Everett Collection, 14, Prisma/Album, 5, The Print Collector Heritage Images, 17, ZUMA Press/ROPI, 15; Shutterstock: Antonio Guillem, 19 (bottom left), BrAt82, cover (bottom right), Chuck Rausin, cover (top left), Early Spring, cover (bottom middle), Everett Historical, 6, Georgios Kollidas, 10, Igor Golovniov, 7, LOVEgraphic, 28, ober-art, 26, POM POM, cover (top right), Sashkin, 2, szefei, 19 (top left), Ukki Studio, cover (top middle), veronchick84, 19 (communications towers), zendograph, cover (bottom left); Wikimedia: Public Domain,
Design Elements: Shutterstock

CONTENTS

Chapter 1: The first words.............................. 4

Chapter 2: Before the telephone 6

Chapter 3: Inventors 10

Chapter 4: How telephones work.................. 18

Chapter 5: Telephones today........................ 24

Timeline 29

Glossary.. 30

Comprehension questions 31

Find out more 31

Websites.. 32

Index... 32

THE FIRST WORDS

"Mr Watson, come here. I want to see you." Scottish-born scientist Alexander Graham Bell said these words to his assistant, Thomas Watson, on 10 March, 1876, in Boston, Massachusetts. Bell and Watson were in different rooms at the time. Bell wanted Watson to help him because he had spilled something on his clothes.

Watson ran to Bell to tell him the good news. Watson had heard Bell's voice through their new machine. Bell's words were the first ever heard through a telephone.

an early version of Bell's telephone in action

Alexander Graham Bell's first demonstration of the telephone took place in Boston, USA.

That same day Bell wrote a letter to his father telling him that the telephone was a great success. He said people would one day be able to talk to each other directly without leaving their homes or sending letters.

2 BEFORE THE TELEPHONE

Before the telephone, most people talked to each other in person. They walked, rode horses or travelled in coaches to visit their friends and family.

People wrote letters to those who lived far away. But post travelled slowly in the 1800s. A letter could take weeks or months to arrive. Letters also cost a lot of money to send.

A Pony Express rider passes a man working on the transcontinental telegraph line, which would later put the Pony Express out of business.

THE PONY EXPRESS

From April 1860 to October 1861, the Pony Express delivered mail and news to the western United States. Riders carried the mail on horseback along the 3,058-kilometre (1,900-mile) route. They changed to fresh horses at stations along the way. It took about 10 days to deliver mail along the route.

POST BY RAIL

In the UK, the first mail coach began travelling between London and Bristol, in 1784. By 1830, a mail train was making deliveries from Liverpool to Manchester.

In the United States, the first train to regularly carry mail travelled on the Baltimore and Ohio Railroad in 1832. By 1838 all US railroads carried mail. Mail clerks sorted letters on the trains as they travelled across the country.

THE TELEGRAPH

This stamp shows one of the first mail coaches in England.

In 1842, American inventor Samuel Morse finished a machine he'd been working on for several years. It was a message-sending device that he called the telegraph. But it would be two years before Morse would find out if his new invention worked. He had to wait until he got the money to build a 61-kilometre (38-mile) long telegraph line between Baltimore and Washington, DC. Once he was able to test the machine, he sent the first telegraph message on 24 May 1844.

Telegraph messages were sent using a system of dots and dashes called Morse code. The messages were tapped out in Morse code on the machine. Then the machine sent the message through wires to another machine that tapped the coded message onto paper.

Telegraphs helped people communicate over long distances, but they had some

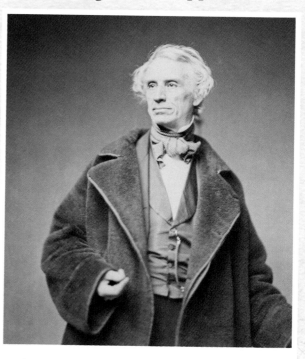

Samuel Morse

problems. For one thing, people didn't have telegraphs in their homes. They had to go to telegraph offices. Plus, most people didn't know Morse code. Telegraph operators had to send and decode the messages, which left no opportunity to send private messages.

Telegraphs could also send only one message at a time, and sometimes they didn't work over very long distances. People needed a better way to communicate with friends and family.

MORSE CODE

Try sending your own messages in Morse code by tapping on a table using the list below. The dots are quick taps, the dashes are longer taps.

A	. --	1	-- -- -- --
B	-- . . .	2	. . -- -- --
C	-- . -- .	3	. . . -- --
D	-- . .	4	. . . . --
E	.	5	. . . . .
F	. . -- .	6	-- . . . .
G	-- -- .	7	-- -- . . .
H	. . . .	8	-- -- -- . .
I	. .	9	-- -- -- -- .
J	. -- -- --	O	-- -- -- -- --
K	-- . --		
L	. -- . .		
M	-- --		
N	-- .		
O	-- -- --		
P	. -- -- .		
Q	-- -- . --		
R	. -- .		
S	. . .		
T	--		
U	. . --		
V	. . . --		
W	. -- --		
X	-- . . --		
Y	-- . -- --		
Z	-- -- . .		

INVENTORS

Technically, the telephone was not invented by just one person. Scientists in Great Britain, France, Germany and the United States all contributed ideas that led to the first telephone.

MICHAEL FARADAY

In 1831, British scientist Michael Faraday was able to make electricity with a wire and a magnet. He also built the first electric motor in the early 1820s.

Before Faraday, many people believed that electricity was a liquid. But Faraday's experiments proved that electricity was a force. It travelled like a wave along different materials at different speeds.

British scientist Michael Faraday

Later, many inventors used Faraday's work with electricity to create their own inventions. People used his ideas about electricity to develop many machines, including the telephone.

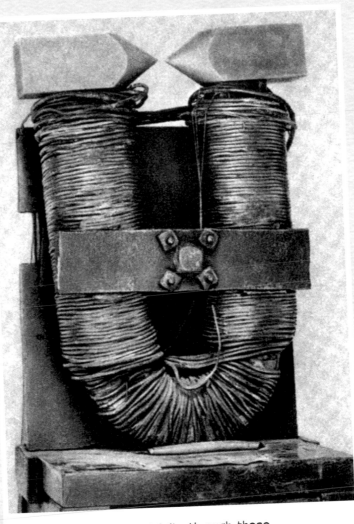

Faraday passed electricity through these metal coils. This made the coils magnetic.

CHARLES BOURSEUL

In 1854, French scientist Charles Bourseul worked for a telegraph company. There he made improvements to Samuel Morse's telegraph system. He was also studying sound. He knew that sound is made by **vibrations**. He believed machines could send and receive these vibrations. In this way, sound could be sent through wires over great distances. Bourseul's ideas encouraged many other inventors to work with sound and electricity.

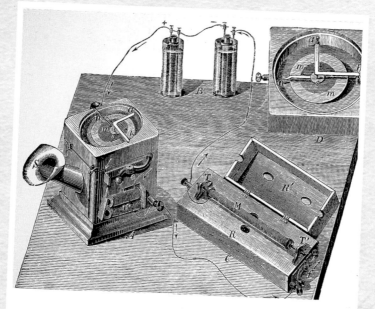

Charles Borseul's ideas about sound paved the way for the invention of the telephone.

vibration trembling motion; musical instruments make vibrations when people play them

Johann Philipp Reis

Between 1860 and 1862, German teacher and inventor Johann Philipp Reis worked on a machine he built that changed sound into electricity. It then sent the electricity as vibrations through a wire. The electricity was changed back into sound at the other end of the wire. Reis called his machine a telephone. But his invention could send only faint sounds, and it was difficult to make out what the voice at the other end was saying.

Johann Philipp Reis' telephone system was the first of its type.

DID YOU KNOW?

Reis' machine was built out of several strange parts, including a carved wooden ear, a knitting needle and a violin. The caller spoke into the wooden ear. Inside the ear, metal parts vibrated, sending vibrations down copper wires that ran into another room. The wire ends were wrapped around a knitting needle that was placed inside the violin. The receiver put his or her ear next to the violin to listen to the vibrations.

GUGLIELMO MARCONI

In the early 1890s, Guglielmo Marconi was working on wireless telegraphy. This was the idea of sending telegraph messages over long distances without wires. The wireless telegraph would instead use radio waves, or electric signals sent through the air. Radio waves are sent and received by an **antenna**.

In 1895 Marconi had a breakthrough. When he raised the height of his antenna, he was able to send radio waves up to 3.2 kilometres (2 miles) away.

The next year Marconi travelled to the UK with his new wireless telegraph machine. In 1897 he sent the first wireless telegraph over water. It travelled across the Bristol Channel from Wales to England.

Italian inventor Guglielmo Marconi

antenna wire or dish that sends or receives radio waves

On 12 December 1901, Marconi sent the world's first wireless telegraph message across the Atlantic from England to Newfoundland in Canada – more than 3,380 kilometres (2,100 miles) away. This completely changed communication. British armed forces began using Marconi's wireless telegraph system during the Boer War (1899–1902) to quickly and easily communicate with military personnel back home. Marconi's system also helped locate ships in distress. When the passenger ship RMS *Titanic* struck an iceberg in 1912, its radio operator used the Marconi system to signal nearby ships for help.

In 1903 Marconi sent a message using his wireless telegraph from President Theodore Roosevelt in the United States to King Edward VII in England.

ALEXANDER GRAHAM BELL

In 1876 Alexander Graham Bell made the first telephone that successfully worked with the human voice. Bell was born in Scotland in 1847 and moved to the United States in the 1870s. He was interested in sound and speech.

At first Bell did not plan to invent a telephone. He was simply trying to improve the telegraph by sending more than one message through a wire at a time. Plus he wanted to send more than Morse code messages. But he also wanted to see if he could send the human voice through the wires.

Bell spent many years building and testing machines. Finally, on 10 March 1876, his machine worked. It sent Bell's voice through wires to another room where his assistant, Thomas Watson, heard him. Bell and Watson kept working on the telephone, and seven months later, they talked to each other from two different towns. Bell's discovery forever changed the way people communicate.

DID YOU KNOW?

At one time, Alexander Graham Bell called his invention the "speaking telegraph".

Alexander Graham Bell invented the telephone in 1876.

4 HOW TELEPHONES WORK

Unlike a mobile phone, a landline telephone needs to be plugged into an electrical outlet in order to work. The telephone changes a person's voice into electrical signals. These signals are sent through a wire to another telephone. This telephone turns the electrical signals back into the person's voice.

A mobile phone also changes a person's voice into electrical signals. But the signals are turned into radio waves. The radio waves are sent to the nearest **communications tower.** The communications tower sends the waves to another mobile phone. The mobile phone changes the radio waves back into electrical signals then back to the caller's voice.

Every telephone has a microphone, a speaker and a keypad. A person presses the numbers on the keypad to call another phone. A **smartphone's** keypad is part of a touchscreen.

WHAT HAPPENS WHEN YOU MAKE A PHONE CALL?

Ever wonder what happens when you make a call on a mobile phone? The infographic below shows what happens when you press the call button on your mobile phone.

Phone A calls Phone B.

Phone A
Phone A scans for the best mobile signal.

A communications tower verifies that mobile Phone A is a valid customer and then checks for available voice channels.

A Mobile Telephone Switching Office (MTSO) contains the equipment for routing mobile phone calls.

The MTSO scans for Phone B globally and locates the strongest mobile signal near Phone B.

Phone B

The MTSO tells the mobile phones which frequencies to use. When the tower and the phones switch to those frequencies, the call is connected. All of this happens in just a few seconds.

communications tower tall pole that houses antennae and other electronic equipment that send and receive radio waves
smartphone mobile phone that performs many of the same jobs as a computer

THE TELEPHONE BECOMES A HOUSEHOLD ITEM

People were very interested in Bell's invention. By the end of 1877, less than two years after they were invented, 3,000 telephones had been **installed** in homes in the United States.

During the 1890s many new telephone lines were installed in countries around the world.

install put in

The number of phones in use grew quickly.
By 1881 nearly 48,000 telephones were in use in the
United States. By 1915 the number had grown to
more than 10 million. At that time, there were only
100 million people living in the United States.

In the UK the National Telephone Company
(NTC) was formed during the 1880s and 1890s.
It combined several
telephone companies into a
national network. The NTC
put up lots of telephone
wires across the UK.
During this time many
people got telephones in
their homes. By 1900 seven
telephone calls were made
for every one telegraph
message that was sent.
The telephone had
quickly become
the favourite way
to communicate.

By 1915 one out of every 10 households
in the United States had a telephone.

"HELLO, OPERATOR?"

By the late 1800s, the first telephone **exchanges** were set up. An exchange connects telephones. In the early years of telephones, operators worked at the exchanges. The operator sat in front of a **switchboard** – a huge box with many wires and switches – that received all telephone calls. When people made a call, they talked to the operator first. The operator connected their phone to the other person's phone. Later, machines were built to work the exchanges.

switchboard operators from the early 1900s

exchange system that connects many telephones
switchboard control centre for connecting the lines of a telephone system

LONG-DISTANCE CALLING

At first telephones only worked over short distances. Then in the late 1800s, long-distance telephone service was developed. The east and west coasts of the United States were connected by telephone in 1915.

In 1927, the first call was made across the Atlantic Ocean. The call connected people in New York City and London. Soon telephone communication spread around the world.

In 1892, Bell made the first long-distance telephone call, from New York City to Chicago.

5 TELEPHONES TODAY

Landline telephones are being used less and less in homes today. Now, more people use mobile phones as their main telephone.

In 1973 American **engineer** Martin Cooper invented the mobile phone. It weighed 1.1 kilograms (2.5 pounds). As **technology** has improved, mobile phones have become smaller and lighter. The technology spread quickly and people all over the world began buying mobile phones. Today, almost two-thirds of the world's population owns a mobile phone.

Martin Cooper shows off the first mobile phone, which he invented in 1973.

engineer person who uses science and maths to plan, design and build things
technology use of science to do practical things, such as designing complex machines

TEXT MESSAGING

Texting has changed the way we communicate. A text is a message a person types into his or her mobile phone to send to another mobile phone. British engineer Neil Papworth used his computer to send the first text message to a mobile phone on 3 December 1992. The message said, "Merry Christmas".

In 1997, Nokia made the first mobile phone with a full keyboard for sending text messages. At first users could only send texts to people on the same mobile phone network. But in 1999 texting became available across all networks. More and more people began sending texts. Now more than 560 billion text messages are sent every month!

The Nokia Communicator was the first mobile phone with a full keyboard.

TEXT SPEAK

Texts let people send short messages from their mobile phones. In response, people developed a new "language" to keep their messages short. Here are some popular "text speak" words:

```
BTW = by the way
LOL = laugh out loud
XOXO = kisses and hugs
```

People also text "smileys" to express their feelings. These include:

```
:) = happy
:( = sad
>:[ = angry
```

DID YOU KNOW?

Japanese inventor Shigetaka Kurita invented the first set of emojis in 1999.

SMARTPHONES

Today, most smartphones are minicomputers. They allow people to connect to the Internet. Smartphones also let people stay connected to friends on social media sites, such as Facebook and Twitter. People can even download **apps** and play games on their phones.

Telephones are an even more important part of everyday life. They help people keep in touch with their jobs, friends and families.

The world's first smartphone was called the Simon Personal Communicator. It was invented in 1992, 15 years before the iPhone.

app useful program that is downloaded to computers and mobile devices; app is short for application

HOW WE USE SMARTPHONES

This infographic shows the average amount of time people spend on different activites on their smartphones. Some people use their phones more for texting, social media and surfing the Internet than for making calls to other people.

OTHER 8%

GAMES 8%

EMAIL 9%

INTERNET 14%

SOCIAL MEDIA 15%

TEXTS 20%

CALLS 26%

TIMELINE

1784	The first mail coach travels between London and Bristol
1830	The UK's first mail train makes deliveries between Liverpool and Manchester
1831	Michael Faraday makes electricity with a wire and a magnet, proving that electricity is a force; he also built the first electric motor in the 1820s
1832	The first train to regularly carry mail travels in the United States
1842	Samuel Morse invents the telegraph and Morse code
1854	Charles Bourseul experiments with sending sound through wires
1860–1861	The Pony Express delivers mail and news to the western United States
1860–1862	Johann Philipp Reis builds a machine that changes sound into electricity, and then sound again; he calls his machine a telephone
1876	Alexander Graham Bell speaks the first words to be heard through a telephone in another room
1877	The Bell Telephone Company installs 3,000 telephones in the United States
1880s	The National Telephone Company is formed in the UK
1897	Guglielmo Marconi sends the first wireless telegraph over water
1915	The east and west coasts of the United States are connected by telephone
1927	The first call is made across the Atlantic Ocean
1973	Martin Cooper invents the mobile phone
1992	Neil Papworth sends the first text message to a mobile phone from his computer
1992	The world's first smartphone, the Simon Personal Communicator, is invented
1997	Nokia is the first company to produce a mobile phone with a full keyboard
1999	Shigetaka Kurita invents the first set of emojis
2007	Apple invents the iPhone, one of the world's most popular smartphones
2017	More than 560 billion text messages are sent every month

GLOSSARY

antenna wire or dish that sends or receives radio waves

app useful program that is downloaded to computers and mobile devices; app is short for application

communications tower tall pole that houses antennae and other electronic equipment that send and receive radio waves

engineer person who uses science and maths to plan, design and build things

exchange system that connects many telephones

install put in

smartphone mobile phone that performs many of the same jobs as a computer

switchboard control centre for connecting the lines of a telephone system

technology use of science to do practical things, such as designing complex machines

vibration trembling motion; musical instruments make vibrations when people play them

COMPREHENSION QUESTIONS

1. Before the telephone was invented, people communicated by travelling to other people's homes. They also sent letters. In what ways have telephones made communicating today easier?

2. Choose two telephones from the book, one early and one modern. Using the text and photos, compare and contrast the two telephones. How has the modern telephone changed from the early one?

3. Today, many people own smartphones. What are the good things about using a smartphone? What are the bad things?

FIND OUT MORE

Alexander Graham Bell (Science Biographies), Catherine Chambers (Raintree, 2014)

Telephones and Mobiles (Technology Timelines), Tom Jackson (Franklin Watts, 2015)

Today's Technology (Infographic How it Works), Jon Richards (Wayland, 2016)

WEBSITES

www.bbc.co.uk/education/clips/z4rtvcw
Find out more about Samuel Morse and the first transatlantic
cable messages.

www.dkfindout.com/uk/science/amazing-inventions/telephone/
Discover how telephone technology has changed over time.

kids.britannica.com/scholars/article/telephone/110260
Learn about the history and development of the telephone.

INDEX

Bell, Alexander Graham 4–5, 16, 17, 20, 23, 29
Bell Telephone Company 29
Boer War 15
Bourseul, Charles 12, 29

Cooper, Martin 24, 29

Edward VII, King 15
electricity 10, 11, 12, 13, 29
electric motor 10, 29
emojis 26, 29

Faraday, Michael 10–11, 29

iPhone 27, 29

Kurita, Shigetaka 26, 29

long-distance calling 23, 29

mail coaches 7, 29
mail trains 7, 29
Marconi, Guglielmo 14–15, 29
mobile phones 18, 24, 25, 26, 28, 29
Mobile Telephone Switching Office (MTSO) 19
Morse code 8, 9, 12, 16, 29
Morse, Samuel 8, 29

National Telephone Company (NTC) 21, 29
Nokia Communicator 25, 29

operators 22

Papworth, Neil 25, 29
Pony Express 6, 29

radio waves 14, 18
Reis, Johann Philipp 13, 29
Roosevelt, Theodore 15

Simon Personal Communicator 27, 29
smartphones 18, 27, 28, 29

telegraph 8–9, 12, 14, 16, 17, 29
texting 25–26, 28, 29
Titanic 15

Watson, Thomas 4, 16
wireless telegraph 14–15, 29